Hickory Bob:
The Bob Harmon Story

To Mark with best wishes
Richard Cooper

Hickory Bob:
The Bob Harmon Story

From Missouri orphan to the Major Leagues
to Louisiana millionaire, Bob Harmon touched
all the bases. The true story of a dead ball era star.

by Richard Cooper

LEATHERS
PUBLISHING

4500 College Boulevard
Overland Park, Kansas 66211
888-888-7696
www.leatherspublishing.com

ALSO BY RICHARD COOPER

Hunting? Don't Forget the Toilet Paper!
(with Don Lamm, Jr.)

To Jack Trost
Without his help, this biography
of his beloved Daddy Bob
would never have been possible

ACKNOWLEDGMENTS

First and foremost, appreciation must be extended to Jack Trost, Jr., the grandson of Bob Harmon, who co-operated fully in answering endless questions during telephone and face to face interviews about his grandfather. His enthusiasm for the undertaking and providing priceless pictures throughout the life of his grandfather became the strong underpinning for the book.

Great-Granddaughter Beth Hart added much to the story with an enthusiasm that even exceeded that of her uncle's, if that is possible.

Nancy Bryant Benton of Tulsa, Oklahoma provided a vast amount of information including tips on where additional facts might be found, nearly all of which turned out to be rewarding gems. Nancy is a distant relative of Bob Harmon. Her grandfather was Bob Harmon's uncle.

The occupant and co-owner of the Harmon plantation home as this book was written was Sherry Nelson. Her interest in the history of the home and its occupants, and willingness to share that information, dovetailed perfectly with the author's undertaking.

It was learned that information contained in the Baseball Hall of Fame & Museum in Cooperstown, New York is not limited to those persons who have been inducted into that institution. The museum portion contains a treasure-trove of data and other information about past stars of the game that can be unlocked with a simple letter of inquiry.

The rare books section of the Ouachita Parish Public Library in Monroe, Louisiana was immensely helpful, especially Larry Foreman and Mary Robison of that institution's staff.

The Monroe Chamber of Commerce spared no time in filling my request for a road map of Ouachita Parish.

The Herbert S. Ford Memorial Museum, Inc. of Homer, Louisiana provided a wealth of information on the oil boom in northwest Louisiana in the early 1920s. Linda Volentine was diligent in performing requested research.

The Shreve Memorial Library of Shreveport, Louisiana was quick to respond to a request for an account of Bob Harmon's finest pitching performance.

Insight was given into the personality and charitable activities of daughter Jean Harmon by the Children's Museum of Lake Charles, Louisiana.

Don Terry of West Monroe, Louisiana graciously offered his services in researching additional Harmon data, reflecting his intense interest in north Louisiana history.

The current owner of the farm where Bob Harmon was born is Bill Bryant. He readily answered inquiries that led to valuable discoveries in the Harmon life.

Bob Douglas, President of the Barton County, Missouri Historical Society, provided vital microfilm evidence from early editions of the Liberal *Enterprise* and Liberal *News*, and added appreciated encouragement throughout the writing of the book.

Drenda Farrell provided the Liberal High School records of 1902, 1903, 1904, and 1905, which she had salvaged from almost certain destruction. It was a find that opened the door to the Harmon school record.

Revealing news articles came from the Monroe *News-Star* and the Shreveport *Times*.

Morrison Printing provided skillful copying of vital photographs and documents.

Career statistics were courtesy of Internet sources Baseball-Reference.com, Baseball-Almanac.com, BaseballLibrary.com, StLouis.Cardinals.mlb.com, Retrosheet.org, and Wikipedia.com.

Melody Metzger Swor did the proof reading of the manuscript with a watchful eye that has been sharpened by her long years with the Lamar *Democrat*.

Sincere appreciation is extended to my wife, Mae, who helped sort and identify countless dozens of old newspaper clippings and tolerated my long hours of writing while other household duties were neglected.

Last, but certainly not least, a sincere thank you to Brian King of the Liberal Historical Society who first planted the idea of writing this biography.

CONTENTS

Prologue

The story of Bob Harmon, his baseball career, and remarkable life that followed is a story that needs to be told. In baseball terms, he started with two strikes against him, a virtual orphan the first day of his life. His success on the diamond was realized through natural talent and unrelenting determination. Determination would serve him well in the years following his baseball career, but a sincere generosity and caring for people were interwoven with it.

Research into his life and career has involved the discovery of isolated bits and pieces of information, a search for additional facts to link them together, placing them in the correct order of occurrence, and tying them together with a logical narrative. Intimate and lengthy discussions with family members and assemblage of the life experiences of the principals of the story have given the author the feeling of being a family member also. It has been a unique experience to see the orphaned infant grow older page after page, to high school student, to aspiring professional athlete, to major league star, to strikingly successful businessman, to elder statesman of Ouachita Parish, Louisiana.

It has been the author's intent to present a factual account of the Harmon life in such a way as to provide informative and enjoyable reading for family members, residents of southwest Missouri and northern Louisiana, and the general reading public.

Any errors in this effort are the author's exclusively.

Chapter 1
THE CONFIRMATION

The muscular and innocent looking young man from Missouri had played baseball before but on a considerably lower level, on what was known as a "town team" in the town of his birth, Liberal, Missouri. He loved the game and had performed quite well the year before with the Whites, also known as the Whitesox.

The scene was a copper mining camp near Morenci, Arizona Territory, about 12 miles from the border with New Mexico Territory. The year was 1907. Theodore Roosevelt was in the midst of his first full term as president and had received the Nobel Peace Prize the year before for his role in helping negotiate the Treaty of Portsmouth ending the Russo-Japanese War.

Bob Harmon was only 19 years old and was a product of small town America having lived the last half of his life on a farm near the small southwest Missouri community that had a population of less than 900. He had attended Liberal High School and was within four weeks of graduation in 1905 when he withdrew to help his parents operate their 48-acre farm. It was a difficult decision for the entire family. Bob had made good grades and had many friends in high school, and his parents placed considerable value on education, especially his father, O. E. (Ellie) Harmon. Ellie Harmon was a widely known learned man having attended college, practiced law in Illinois, and lectured as a respected amateur astronomer. He had a large library and spent many hours reading the classics. Poetry was one of his favorite pastimes, both reading verse and writing his own. As Ellie's health began to fail, the help of a young and strong son became increasingly important in operating the Harmon farm.

Bob was honored when some of his fellow workers asked if he wanted to try out for the company team in the spring of 1907. He had some concerns about competing on a considerably higher level of play, but bolstering his confidence was the fact that he had been one of the stars of the Liberal Whitesox. Pitching was his strength, but he also had been a feared hitter, batting from both sides and usually hitting in the lead off spot, a most uncommon place in the lineup for a pitcher.

It should be noted that baseball was a dominant and closely followed sport in small town America in the early twentieth century, and player skill was remarkably high. Many major leaguers got their start there, and Bob Harmon was one of them. It seems likely that others on that Liberal team of 1906 could have made it to the major leagues if they had persisted. However, only Bob Harmon with a strong right arm and intense determination made it.

To overcome his apprehension when asked to try out for the company team, he worked on improving his delivery, adding a high kick with his left leg and an overhead delivery of a blazing fast ball. When it was his turn to show what he could do, it quickly became apparent that he could compete at Morenci. He knew then that his future was in baseball. He lacked control, but surely that would come with time.

Chapter 2
LYRIAN FARM & TRAGEDY

Cora Rachel Noyes married Frank Greene on March 30, 1886, in Junction City, Kansas and quickly found that life would not be dull as the wife of a traveling man. Frank was active in politics in Kansas and for a time was employed by the Union Pacific Railroad. He was the traveling spokesman for the Anti-Monopoly Party in Kansas, trying to convince the populace of the evils of the "Robber Barons" of big business. The Anti-Monopoly Party sought to promote the interests of the working classes and was much in harmony with the Greenback Party and the Knights of Labor, although the once-large labor organization was by this time dying. The Anti-Monopoly Party was also showing signs of fading. The Populist Party was becoming the rising political force on the Great Plains of America.

Cora traveled with her husband much of the time, staying in hotels in Hutchinson, Beloit, Wichita, Topeka, and other cities in Kansas as well as Chester, Lincoln, and Omaha, Nebraska. However, when she became pregnant, the rigors of living out of a suitcase and moving to three or four different cities in a week would soon become more taxing than her slight frame could withstand. As Frank continued his seemingly endless tour of speaking engagements for the

Anti-Monopolists, Cora retired to her parents' home, which was on a 48-acre farm, one and one-half miles southeast of Liberal. Her parents were James A. Noyes and Caroline Atwell Noyes.

At this time, Viola and Ellie Harmon were living in Chehalis, Washington where they had moved from Illinois in about 1881. However, Viola came back to Liberal as she felt she should be at her sister's side when the baby was born. That event occurred late in the day of October 15, 1887, with the birth of a healthy boy. However, for Cora it was a difficult delivery that left her weakened from long hours of labor and loss of blood. Her condition worsened during the night, and she died early the following morning.

For Viola Harmon, who had no children of her own, the decision on who should take care of the newborn infant came quickly. Frank, who was not present for the birth, was almost constantly on the road and was in no position to care for his son. Therefore, Viola sent a telegram to Ellie in Chehalis informing him that they had a nephew to be raised as their own son. It would be their second chance at parenthood since they had lost a son at the age of eight months about three years before.

The infant was named Robert, and exactly how long Viola stayed at the farm with him is not clear. It was at least a year before she and young Robert headed west to rejoin Ellie in Chehalis.

The farm southeast of Liberal was to become Ellie Harmon's favorite place on earth. He would name it "Lyrian Farm," and it would become a sanctuary for him when he and Viola relocated there in the spring of 1897 after his health began to show signs of deterioration about a year earlier. They purchased the farm from Viola's parents, although only Viola's name appears as the grantee of the property. Viola and Ellie would make Lyrian Farm their home until his death from Parkinson's Disease in late August 1940.

When the Harmons settled on Lyrian Farm in 1897, foster son Robert was then approaching age 10, and they loved him as though he was their biological son. However, there is no evidence to show he was ever legally adopted. Nevertheless, by this time the youngster had taken Harmon as his surname, and Greene conveniently became his middle name.

Bob Harmon would attend five years of schooling in a typical southwest Missouri one-room country school and two-and-three-quarters years at Liberal High School before making the difficult decision to withdraw and work full time on his parents' farm. He stayed with farming for nearly two years and played baseball with the local Whitesox in his spare time in the summer months. When Ellie elected to discontinue farming and rent out his land to someone else, Bob was free to pursue his ambition to return to the West. He had earlier passed up an opportunity to work in the copper mines of Arizona and make what was good money for a young man of 19. Now was his chance, and he boarded a train for the Great Southwest to seek what he hoped would be his fortune. What he found there was far different from life in Liberal, and the landscape represented a world he had never seen before, not even during his return to Liberal from Chehalis in 1897. He would work long hard hours in the Morenci copper mine, but mining eventually came to have only an incidental connection with his life there. Baseball became the driving force of his existence, and the pursuit of the mythical fortune would have to wait. It would eventually come nearly two decades later, but not in Arizona and not in baseball.

Chapter 3
THROWING HEAT AT MORENCI
AND
GRADUATION TO THE PRO RANKS

When the spring of 1907 arrived, 19-year-old Bob Harmon was ready to try out as a pitcher. He had worked out during the winter when not on the job and had developed a high kick and overhead delivery that resulted in what can only be described as "throwing heat." He didn't bother with other deliveries or a change of speed. It was just heat followed by more heat and still more heat. His strong right arm held up well, and he found that he could blow pitch after pitch by nearly all the hitters that his company team would encounter. There was the problem of control, however, and it plagued him all during the 1907 season; it was a problem that he was going to have to cope with. In reality, it was a problem that would sporadically plague him during his entire baseball career.

Playing on a company team was considered independent or semi-pro ball, and most such teams kept no records of players' hitting, pitching, or fielding statistics. The only thing from Bob Harmon's 1907 season at Morenci that has survived is an account of his striking out 146 batters in 12 consecutive games. That is an average of nearly two strikeouts per inning through that string of games. The heat was working.

During the autumn and early winter of late 1907, he corresponded with a number of professional teams, deciding that he did indeed have a future in baseball. It would mean gambling with his future by quitting his job with the copper mine, but he had made somewhat of a gamble before when he left high school prior to graduation to work on his parents' farm. However, that was more of a fulfillment of an obligation than it was a gamble. It seemed that he had landed the big fish in his search for a minor league team when Portland (Ore.) of the Pacific Coast League indicated they would allow him to try out. April of 1908 found him in a Portland uniform, ready to try his blazing speed on a high caliber of minor league competition. How much trouble Pacific Coast League hitters would have had with his pitching cannot be determined because his wildness ended his trial at five games when Portland cut him from their roster. He was not ready for that level of play, and he knew that improving his control would include a better grip on his nerves before success could be achieved on any level of the pro game.

He had received some previous feelers from the Waterloo Cubs of the Iowa State League so he contacted that club to see if there was still some interest. When he learned that there was, he packed his belongings and scraped together enough money for a ticket to Waterloo. Things began to come together there, and he spent most of the 1908 season with Waterloo compiling a won-loss record of 14-10. He struck out 85 and limited bases on balls to 63. Finally, he was gaining a sense of control.

Near the end of the season he hooked onto Freeport of the Wisconsin-Illinois League. Only a few games remained, but it gave him an opportunity to pitch to batters of a slightly higher level. However, Freeport was not exactly known as a baseball town. Tucked away in the northwestern corner of Illinois, its principal claim to fame was serving as one of the sites for the famous Lincoln-Douglas debates of 1858.

Where the aspiring young righthander spent the off-season of 1908-09 is not clear, but he was determined to move up the minor league ladder. He scored a coup of sorts when the Shreveport Pirates of the Texas League expressed an interest. It was there that he would pitch the finest game of his career, and that would open the door to the major leagues.

Chapter 4

THE SHREVEPORT GEM

The Harmon career at Shreveport would last through only 16 appearances involving a total of 94 innings pitched. His won-loss record was 5-3 with 82 strikeouts, just 24 bases on balls, and an impressive earned run average of just 1.77. Bob Harmon was developing into a crafty and confident pitcher, but he still relied most heavily on a blazing fastball.

The sports section of the May 11, 1909, edition of the Shreveport *Times* led with the following headline, "Runless, Hitless Game for Harmon." Not only did he set down visiting Galveston 6-0 without a hit, he also had a perfect game going into the seventh. With one out in that inning, Yohe of Galveston weakly dumped a grounder down the third base line that Bob immediately pounced on. Along with his outstanding fastball, he was gaining a reputation as a fine fielding pitcher. However, for one painful moment in that seventh frame, he couldn't get a grip on the ball and juggled it. When he did make the throw to first, Yohe had crossed the bag, an error was charged, and the perfect game fell by the wayside.

Yohe was the only batter to get on base as Harmon retired the next eight hitters to cement his near-perfect gem.

No-hitters in the minor leagues immediately get the attention of major league management whether in today's majors or the majors of Bob Harmon's time. Nowhere was help needed as badly in either league as the hapless St. Louis Cardinal franchise of the National League. In 1908, the Cardinals finished dead last for the second consecutive season and were only one rung above the cellar in 1906. All three seasons had been under the management of John McCloskey.

McCloskey was fired shortly after the end of the 1908 season, and the Cardinals went shopping for a replacement. On December 12, 1908, they acquired veteran catcher Roger Bresnahan from the New York Giants in exchange for three Cardinal players, Red Murray, Bugs Raymond, and Admiral Schlei. Bresnahan was a durable catcher who could also play on the infield when needed, and generally hit in the .280s. However, the Cardinal front office was more interested in him for leadership and installed him as the player-manager for the 1909 season. Bresnahan would be faced with the difficult task of rebuilding a team that lost 105 games the season before, and hadn't finished in the first division since 1901.

Bob Harmon's masterpiece at Shreveport got the immediate attention of the Cardinal front office. Bresnahan urged strengthening the pitching staff, and with that recommendation the Cardinals offered Shreveport $3,500 for Harmon's contract, which was accepted. It was to be on a trial basis, with the Cardinals reserving the right to return him if not satisfied with his work on the mound. Harmon showed enough promise that Bresnahan decided to keep him. A $3,500 price tag in 1909 would be the equivalent of about $75,000 in 2007.

Exactly how many more mound appearances Harmon made for Shreveport is not certain, but it surely must have been few or none. He pitched the Texas League no-hitter on May 10, and on June 23 he was on the mound for the Cardinals at St. Louis' League Park.

His rookie year was tough, being taken from the minors and immediately thrown into a starting role in the majors. All together he started 17 games (10 were complete games), relieved in four, and pitched a total of 159 innings. His won-loss record was 6-11. Not exactly impressive statistics, but they didn't accurately reveal the pitcher behind those statistics. Bresnahan saw some things that convinced him the 21-year-old Missouri righthander had the potential of becoming a future Cardinal star. One was obvious to everyone when he pitched a full 16 innings to register a 4-3 victory over John McGraw's New York Giants on July 19, while holding the Giants scoreless from the fourth inning on. A short time later he hurled a two-hitter against the Brooklyn Superbas (later Dodgers), losing 1-0 when a Cardinal infield error allowed the sole run to score. Also, his 3.68 ERA didn't go unnoticed. Bob Harmon would definitely be around for the 1910 season.

With almost a complete season under his belt, Harmon would become one of the workhorses in the Cardinal rotation in 1910. He would start 33 games, almost double the starting assignments of his rookie year, and he would complete 15 of them. However, control problems would surface again. In fact, they were never far below the surface throughout his entire baseball career. He would earn the dubious honor of leading the National League in 1910 in bases on balls (133), wild pitches (12), and earned runs (117). The latter figure forced his ERA to an unimpressive 4.46. In the 43 games in which he appeared, his strikeouts totaled 87. His won-loss record was13-15.

However, it would not be entirely fair to judge Bob Harmon on these figures alone. He was pitching for a team mired deep in the second division that had finished no higher than fifth place since 1904, and hadn't had a .500 season since

1901. The support he got at the plate was woefully limited. Roger Bresnahan's rebuilding program was turning out to be an awfully steep hill to climb, but he knew that Bob Harmon had to be an important part of it. The 1911 season would see remarkable progress.

Chapter 5

THE WATERSHED YEAR, 1911

Roger Bresnahan's rebuilding efforts with the Cardinals began to show positive results in 1911 as the team posted a fifth place finish, one game above .500. Much of the Cardinal success can be credited to Bob Harmon, who became the team's leading pitcher, following a workhorse schedule in the starting rotation. He started 41 games that still stands as the franchise record and is likely never to be broken since the major leagues have adopted a policy over the last 25 to 30 years of more carefully counting pitches. Now, when a pitcher approaches 100 pitches, he is likely to be removed for a middle-innings reliever or a closer even if he is pitching a shutout. Few complete games are registered, with the only certainty of a complete game being if the pitcher is working on a no-hitter. Bob Harmon hurled 28 complete games in 1911 and appeared in a total of 51. His ERA dropped to 3.13, and his won-loss record of 23-16 was among the best in the National League.

Harmon developed a mild rivalry with the New York Giants righthander, Christy Mathewson, who was arguably the greatest righthander in the history of the National League and possibly all of baseball. There are some who would rate him as the greatest of all time, throwing from either side. On June 17, 1911, Harmon hooked up with Mathewson in a tight pitcher's duel in which both went the distance, St. Louis winning, 2-1. Harmon allowed just three hits while Matty was touched for only two. It was a satisfying victory for the 23-year-old Cardinal, besting the league's top hurler who was on his way to pitching the Giants into the World Series.

Few pitchers can be equated with Christy Mathewson, but a comparison of the 1911 season's statistics of Matty and Bob Harmon offer some points of interest. Mathewson worked 307 innings with an ERA of 1.99 (lowest in the National League), and a won-loss record of 26-13. Harmon worked more innings, 348, with an ERA of 3.13 and a won-loss record of 23-16. Matty was in the 12th season of his 17-year career at the age of 31. Harmon was in the third season of a nine-year career at age 23.

When asked several times during and after his career his personal choice as baseball's greatest pitcher, Bob Harmon always responded with Walter Johnson. Bob never opposed the "Big Train" since Johnson's 21-year career was entirely in the American League. Coincidentally, the two men were exactly the same age.

Harmon's stellar season also helped to boost attendance which had been flagging for several years. From a season's total of 355,668 in 1910, fifth in the National League, the 1911 numbers swelled to 447,768, third in the league, and the highest since Robison Field opened in 1892. It would remain the Cardinal attendance record until the season of 1926.

Robison Field was the Cardinal's home ballpark for almost 29 years, during which it bore several names. When it opened, it was called New Sportsman's Park, a reference to an older stadium that the Cardinals had occupied in the years they were known as the Brown Stockings. When the Robison brothers, Emmet Stanley and Frank, bought the club in 1899, it simply became League Park, a name it bore through the 1910 season. When the surviving brother, Emmet Stanley, died in 1911, the team was inherited by his niece, Helene Hathaway Robison Britton. She changed the name of the ballpark to Robison Field as a memorial to her father and uncle. It would bear that name until Mrs. Britton sold the team to St. Louis interests in 1917, and Branch Rickey was named club president. During its final three years, 1918 to mid-1920, it was frequently called Cardinal Field. The Cardinals played their last game on the turf of the multi-named Robison Field on June 6, 1920. With its sale for financial reasons, the team moved back to"Old" Sportsman's Park, which by then was owned by the American League St. Louis Browns. The Cardinals would eventually come to own Sportsman's Park and continue to play there until May 8, 1966. It would be stripped of its original name when the team was purchased by August Busch in 1953 and renamed as the first of three Busch Stadiums.

A problem that plagued Robison Field and most baseball parks of its time was frequent fires. The mostly wooden structures were easy victims of stray sparks and carelessness. Robison Field experienced no less than six fires during the first 10 years after it was opened, one during a game on May 4, 1901.

During the 1911 season, *The Sporting News* took note of Harmon's advancement to the top of the Cardinal staff with a quote from manager Roger Bresnahan. "Bresnahan considers him one of the best and speediest young pitchers in America. Harmon is a fine fielding pitcher, being intelligent and having all the ear marks of a comer." This is particularly insightful, coming from Bresnahan who inserted himself into the lineup in 77 games as catcher in 1911. As often as not, Harmon was working with his own field boss behind the plate.

While Bob Harmon was working his way to the top of the Cardinal rotation in 1911, Detroit's "Georgia Peach," Ty Cobb, was on a tear in the American League, hitting safely in 40 consecutive games to set a new mark that would stand for 11 years until surpassed by George Sisler of the St. Louis Browns with 41.

Still the control problem persisted, and it led to establishing two season marks in the National League for 1911 that Harmon would much rather not have had. He led the league in bases on balls with 181 and in earned runs with 121. So many earned runs and still a season ERA of 3.13, show how heavily the Cardinal manager relied on him for mound duty.

Harmon's 1911 performance for St. Louis won him six votes out of a possible 64 for the Chalmers Award, which marked the beginning of what is today known as the Most Valuable Player (MVP) in each league. The National League winner that year was Wildfire Schulte of the Chicago Cubs, while the American League winner was Ty Cobb. The Chalmers Award was named for the Chalmers Automobile Company that donated an automobile to each league's batting average champion, starting in 1910. However, in 1911 Chalmers widened its scope to include a player's overall contribution to his team's success and based its selections on the recommendations of a panel of 11 sportswriters. This recognition would continue through the 1914 season, but would be dropped at that time amid controversy that had arisen over the Chalmers rule that a player would be allowed to win the award only once. For eight years there would be no awards, until the American League revived an MVP award in 1922, and the National League followed suit in 1924. Still, the Chalmers rule persisted with no player allowed more than one league MVP award. This continued to create dissatisfaction that the most genuinely valuable players could likely be passed over because of the rule. The outpouring of criticism seemed to reach a peak when Babe Ruth was denied the 1927 American League MVP, even though he hit 60 home runs, batted .356, and led the Yankees' "Murderer's Row" to the pennant. He was disqualified because he had received the league's award in 1923. Instead, the award went to Yankee first baseman Lou Gehrig, not quite the stature or flamboyant equal of the Bambino but still an imposing power hitter who devastated American League pitchers with 175 runs batted in during that memorable year. He batted number four in the lineup right behind the Babe who was frequently given intentional walks. Finally, the objectionable Chalmers rule was discarded in 1929, in time to allow Rogers Hornsby to collect his second National League MVP as the second baseman of the Chicago Cubs. He had won his first in 1925 with the Cardinals. No MVP awards were given in 1930, but the recognition was revived in 1931 by the Baseball Writers Association of America (BBWAA) who have overseen it to the present.

Sports writers were impressed by the Harmon speed. It became readily apparent in a "field day" held during the traditional post-season series with the crosstown Browns in 1912. Bob won the 100 yard competition with a time of 10 2/5 seconds wearing a full baseball uniform. Sports writers commented about his "long and splendid stride."

After Bob Harmon's stellar season of 1911, he turned in a .500 season in 1912 with a record of 18-18. He was still the workhorse of the staff, starting 34 games and pitching 268 innings. The Cards slipped one place in the end-of-season standings to number six at 63-90, and the Harmon ERA edged up to 3.93. It was apparent that the Roger Bresnahan rebuilding program was losing its momentum.

The 1913 season was an even greater disappointment as the Cardinals slipped two more rungs to end in the National League cellar. There were few bright spots, but Bob Harmon figured in one of them. On May 20, his on-again, off-again rivalry with the Giants' Christy Mathewson once more flashed into view at New York's Polo Grounds as he pitched a two-hit gem to shut out the Giants, 8-0. The Cardinals drove Mathewson to the showers after six innings with 11 hits and a 4-0 lead. However, Matty avenged the loss slightly over a month later when he allowed four hits and two walks in out pitching Bob, 4-0, at Robison Field.

In early June, the Cardinal front office reached a decision to change field managers. Bresnahan was dealt to the Chicago Cubs in a straight cash deal, and second baseman Miller Huggins was elevated to player-manager. Huggins had been a teammate of Harmon's for four years, coming to the Cardinals in 1910. It would be Huggins' undesirable role to be at the helm when the Cardinals finished the season dead last at 51-99. The following season, 1914, Huggins guided the Cardinals above .500 (82-71) and a third place finish. Not until 1917 would the Cardinals climb above .500 again. At that point, the New York Yankees hired Huggins as field manager and put him in charge of what soon became a growing giant. In 12 seasons at the Yankee helm, Huggins would produce six pennants and three World Series titles. He would have the distinction of presiding over the Yankees' Murderer's Row of 1927, arguably the greatest team in the history of baseball. Bob Harmon's record for that disastrous Cardinal season of 1913 was 8-21; yet his ERA was almost identical to the year before at 3.92.

Another bright spot for Bob Harmon in 1913 was only coincidentally connected with baseball, but it occurred during the traditional post season City Series with the crosstown St. Louis Browns of the American League. The two teams would hook up for a preseason best of seven series in early April and a second best of seven in early October. Such a start and conclusion wrapped around the official baseball season in St. Louis was designed to stimulate baseball interest in the city and to increase annual attendance at the clubs' two parks, the Cardinals' Robison Field and the Browns' Sportsman's Park. By 1913, attendance was beginning to dwindle, especially in the October series. Bob had been courting Beulah Gary Mysonhimer, the daughter of a St. Louis preacher, and they planned their wedding for October 11. They knew the date would be during the fall City Series, but took this into account and set the wedding for 8:00 p.m. However, a double header was scheduled for that day, a Saturday, and Manager Huggins complicated the wedding plans by assigning the starting role in the second game to Harmon. The games moved slowly, especially the second game in Bob's mind, and the last out giving a complete game victory to the impending bridegroom came in the fading autumn twilight before only a few scattered fans. There were no lights in those days. It would be nearly 22 years before the Major Leagues would play their first night game. The St. Louis *Post-Dispatch* described Harmon's scramble to get to the church on time.

"Bob Harmon, the Cardinals' big righthander, was married Saturday night, October 11, at St. Paul's Church in St. Louis, to Miss Beulah Mysonhimer. Bob had to hustle some to prevent his bride from being kept waiting at the church. When he had retired the last Brownie in the second game of Saturday's double header in the St. Louis city series it was dusk. Harmon took a shower bath, dressed in a hurry, hopped into his auto and broke the speed laws getting to his apartment. Once there, he slipped into evening dress and hopped into his machine again. Bob reached the church a few minutes before 8 o'clock, the hour set for the ceremony."

Bob was 25 at the time; Beulah was 22. They had met three years before and were engaged several months prior to the ceremony. Their marriage would last 48 years until Bob's death in 1961. All indications are that the marriage was immensely happy until well after his retirement from baseball. However, the relationship became strained during its later years according to family members. Nevertheless, Bob and Beulah remained together throughout.

Much earlier in the year Bob was the victim of a mistaken identity incident. He was arrested and held for a half hour at the Dayton Street police station. Friends came to his rescue, and the police profusely apologized for the mistake.

A last place finish in 1913 made it clear to the Cardinal front office that major changes had to be made. Discussions about possible trades had gone on between the Cardinals and Pittsburgh Pirates for several years, and it was determined that this was the time to make the move. On December 12, 1913, a seven-player swap was made, and Bob Harmon learned that he was going to Pittsburgh.

Chapter 6
THE PITTSBURGH YEARS

The seven-player deal that sent Bob Harmon to the Pirates also involved teammates Ed Konetchy and Mike Mowrey. Konetchy, a skilled first baseman, had been the subject of discussions between the two franchises for several years. In seven seasons with the Cardinals, he had hit close to .300, and the Pirates felt that his acquisition should put the first base side of the Pirates' infield in good hands. Mowrey was a weak hitting but slick fielding third baseman. With him and Konetchy at the corners, the Pirates envisioned an impervious infield built around their great shortstop, Honus Wagner. Harmon would provide the strong pitching that the Pirates' management hoped would propel the team into the National League's first division. In return, the Cardinals got first baseman Dots Miller, infielder Art Butler, outfielder Chief Wilson, and lefthanded pitcher Hank Robinson, who had a good season in 1913 posting a 14-9 won-loss record with an impressive ERA of 2.38. It looked as though the Cardinals may have gotten the better deal, seeing that Pittsburgh wanted Konetchy so badly.

They may have, but not because of Robinson. He played two disappointing years with the Cardinals and was then shipped off to the New York Yankees. Butler was a disappointment also, playing three seasons in which he never hit higher than .254 and retiring at the age of 28. Miller had been one of the heroes of Pittsburgh's 1909 World Series champions and played five credible seasons at every position on the Cardinal infield. Wilson roamed the St. Louis outfield for just three seasons.

Bob Harmon turned out to be the only bright spot on Pittsburgh's side of the transaction as Konetchy and Mowrey were sent to the minors at the end of the 1914 season. That year, "Hickory Bob" would assume the role of one of the hardest working pitchers on the Pirate staff, pitching in 37 games, of which he started 30 with 19 being complete games. His won-loss record was 13-17 with an impressive ERA of 2.53. All of this with a team that finished next to last in the league at 69-85. Only lefty Wilbur Cooper would win more games for the Pirates that year, 16-15. Righthanders Babe Adams and George McQuillan posted almost identical records as that of Harmon. Adams finished 13-16, and McQuillin 13-17. It would turn out to be a slightly built and hardly known righthander, Al Mamaux, who would emerge the following year to team up with Bob Harmon to form a feared duo on the Pirate pitching staff for the next two seasons.

As Harmon was settling into his first season with the Pirates, an assassination in late June in the Balkan city of Sarajevo, Bosnia would lead to a chain reaction of events that would culminate in the Great War, later to be known as World War I.

The nickname "Hickory Bob" came about because of his love of camping, which was an off-season pastime pursued primarily in the foothills of the Ozark Mountains of Missouri. To fuel his campfires, he cut lots of firewood, and in southern Missouri there was and still is an abundance of hickory. At least two purposes were served by such vigorous activity, fuel obviously, but also an excellent means of conditioning for his upper body. According to a family member, so much wood was cut that at times a third benefit was realized, which was additional income.

The passion for camping was undoubtedly acquired during his youth while living in the state of Washington and later in Missouri. It appears that Beulah also loved the outdoors, and the two of them enjoyed camping together for many years. After being sold to Pittsburgh and shortly thereafter purchasing a farm near Homer, Louisiana, the Harmons off-season camping was mostly in Louisiana. By this time the nickname was firmly in place, and it would follow him for the rest of his playing days and occasionally reappear during his post baseball years.

Harmon's 1915 season was his busiest with the Pirates, starting 32 games, winning half of them, pitching 25 complete games, and finishing with an impressive ERA of 2.50. Although both he and the Pirates finished under .500, the team still managed to climb to fifth place, two rungs higher than the preceding season. Harmon's won-loss record was 16-17, and the team record was 73-81.

The season of 1915 marked Bob Harmon's seventh in the majors, and he was now 27 years old. Sports writers began to refer to him as a veteran, and the title of Hickory Bob occasionally became Old Hickory. He was a much more seasoned and crafty pitcher by then, adding a variety of speeds to his curve ball and even throwing an occasional knuckler.

On the sports pages, Bob was overshadowed that season by the young righthander Al Mamaux, who hit his stride and posted an impressive record of 21-8 with an ERA of 2.04. The two of them represented the core of strength of the Pirates' pitching staff. Their combined total of 37 victories made up half of the team's victories that season. When they were paired as starters in a doubleheader, it was likely to be a long afternoon of frustration for the opposing batters. For example, on August 7, 1915, the Pirates swept a double-header from their intrastate rivals, the Philadelphia Phillies. Mamaux won the first game, 6-0, and Harmon followed with a 9-0 shutout.

An examination of statistics shows that Harmon actually was called on for more mound work by manager Fred Clarke in 1915 than was Mamaux. Mamaux hurled 251 innings while Harmon worked 269. Mamaux started 31 games going the route in 17 of them while Harmon started 32 games and completed 25. Only in the ERA column did Mamaux have an edge.

The 1915 season was Fred Clarke's 16th and final one managing the Bucs, retiring after the final game at age 42. For Clarke, it was the end of a superb 21-year career as an outfielder and player/manager. He had guided the Pirates to pennants in 1901, '02, '03, and '09, with the 1909 season also producing a World Series championship. In 1945, Clarke was inducted into the Baseball Hall of Fame.

By 1915, the women's rights movement was several decades old and was focusing on the right to vote as a means of obtaining those rights. The war in Europe was nearly a year old when a German U-boat sank the British passenger liner, Lusitania, on May 6, taking the lives of 128 Americans. Tensions between the U. S. and Germany rose perceptibly. Women's suffrage was gaining momentum, and after Colorado granted the franchise in 1897, the movement had achieved success in 12 states by 1914. Many groups and organizations espoused the cause and sponsored activities of support that included appearances by prominent public figures. One of the celebrities was 54-year-old actress and singer, Lillian Russell. A Pittsburgh newspaper described her appearance at Suffragist Day activities at the Pirates' Forbes Field, September 16, 1915.

It was suffragist day at Forbes Field, the walls of which were decorated with crossed emblems of the party, alternating with crossed American flags. Lillian Russell threw out the first ball, and when Bob Harmon had thrown it over the plate to George Burns, the first batsman, Umpire Rigler, taking off his cap, presented the little white globe to Lillian. His polite bow had nothing on that of John McGraw, when he shook hands with her. Before the game began, the two teams in double file marched on the field carrying yellow balloons. The suffragists not only applauded each good play, but paid $5 for each run. The Giants lost no time in showing their appreciation by taking the lead in the first inning and easily winning 8 to 4.

It is unusually coincidental that Bob Harmon and Al Mamaux should pitch so brilliantly in 1915 but two years later would all but disappear from the baseball scene. The 1916 season began the slide, with Harmon dropping to an 8-11 record and an ERA of 2.81. He started only 17 games and completed just 10. Mamaux turned in another 21-victory season but was the losing pitcher 15 times with an ERA that inched up to 2.53. In 1917, both would encounter disaster. Mamaux would post a record of only 2-11 and an ERA that ballooned to 5.25. He would be traded to Brooklyn the following year. Harmon would not play a game in 1917.

Hickory Bob was becoming increasingly dissatisfied with the Pittsburgh front office as his performance level slipped. He was especially nettled by the Pirates' requirement that the team play a number of post season exhibition games. After the regular season ended in 1916, he joined with several other Pirate players in a rebellion against the requirement and refused to play. The rebellion was doomed to failure since all were under contract to the Pirates and could play for no one else. Finally, in February 1917, he was released to Columbus of the American Association, but a clause in his Pittsburgh contract bound him to the Pirates if he should ever return to the majors. Harmon never reported to Columbus and sat out the entire 1917 season on the farm he had purchased in 1913 in northwest Louisiana near Homer. Oil had already been discovered on the property, and Bob's interest was shifting away from baseball.

However, when the spring of 1918 arrived, the desire to don a pair of spikes and step onto the mound surged again through his veins. After all, he was only 30 and was still in excellent physical condition. His love of dancing had seen to that. Harmon returned to the Pirates for what turned out to be his final fling in the majors. In 1918, he appeared in 16 games, nine of them as a starter, and recorded five complete games. Ironically, his final major league game was on the same field where his career had started, St. Louis' Robison Field, June 28. He faced young Cardinal righthander Lee Meadows and lost 8-1, giving him a final won-loss record of 2-7.

The Pirates relegated him to the minors in the hope that he could somehow regain the effectiveness he had possessed in 1914 and '15. During the remainder of the 1918 season and those of 1919 and 1920, Harmon toiled in the minor leagues in pursuit of the fine edge he once had, but it could not be regained. Also, the attraction of Louisiana and all of its promise became the dominant factor in determining his future. His 13 years in professional baseball were over.

Bob Harmon remained under contract to the Pittsburgh Pirates for two more years until given his final release on December 19, 1922. The release document was signed by club president, Barney Dreyfuss.

During his nine-year major league career, Harmon compiled a won-loss record of 107 victories and 133 losses. He pitched 2,054 innings, striking out 634 batters, while compiling a lifetime ERA of a respectable 3.33. Control became much less of as problem in the final years of his career as he began to rely more heavily on craftiness in his pitching selection. For his entire major league career, he issued 762 bases-on-balls, an average of one walk for every 2 2/3 innings.

Although he was an outstanding hitter during his youth playing with the Liberal Whitesox, that attribute did not follow Bob Harmon to the major leagues. He was a switch hitter, but that didn't seem to offer much help. His lifetime batting average was .184, and the season producing his highest average was 1913 with St. Louis when he hit .261. He struck out 191 times. He hit only one home run, with the Pirates in 1914. Possibly that home run figured in Pittsburgh manager Fred Clarke's decision to insert Harmon into the lineup later in the same season as a pinch hitter, the only time he was ever called on to fill that role. Bob lived up to his manager's confidence, hitting a double to drive in three runs. Surely that was one of the high points of his career at the plate.

His and other pitchers' ineffectiveness at the plate was addressed by Harmon a few years after his retirement from baseball. At a party he attended along with Pirate executive Barney Dreyfuss, with whom he remained friends for many years, Harmon expressed support for a rule change that would allow pinch hitters to bat for pitchers without requiring the pitchers to leave the game. The Shreveport *Times* reported Harmon's remarks in the middle 1920s.

Bob Harmon, retired pitcher, who formerly starred with the Pirates, still finds time while living on his large plantation, to keep posted about baseball affairs. The fiddler while fanning with Barney Dreyfuss this evening made it known that he thinks John Heydler made a wise suggestion last winter when he advocated a measure that would permit pinch-hitters to bat for pitchers without removing the latter from the box. "There are two ways of looking at every question," says Harmon, "but the crowd always gets sore when a pitcher is allowed to hit with runners on base and his team behind. If he gets a hit and then has to run the bases, especially when it is late in the game and he is already feeling the strain from tight pitching, the chances are that the extra exertion will cause him to crack, and the opposition is likely to land on him and defeat him. By all means try out the Heydler suggestion, or even try out the plan of letting eight players do all the batting and excuse the pitcher, whether he likes it or not. The idea is to please the public, and I'm sure this would do it."

This idea was ahead of its time by nearly 50 years. Today, it is a reality in the American League with the designated hitter rule.

Bob Harmon made another observation about baseball that seems to have been ahead of its time when he was a member of the Cardinals. At the end of the 1912 season on September 30, he was invited to participate in a lecture entitled "Inside Baseball" before the Men's Brotherhood of Grace at a St. Louis Presbyterian church. In his remarks, he stated, "Baseball is a business, pure and simple." It would be decades before club owners would come to admit the truth of this statement.

Chapter 7

STRIKING IT RICH IN OIL

W hen Bob Harmon went west to work in the Arizona copper mines in 1907, he did so to make his fortune, or at least to earn an attractive wage compared to what could be earned farming a small acreage in southwest Missouri. When baseball became the dominant force in his life, his route to that fortune was skewed considerably. It didn't offer a fortune, but it was still considerably more money than he had earned before in his life. His 1912 contract with the Cardinals was for an annual salary of $4,800, a comfortable income for that time. That translates into 2007 dollars as approximately $102,000.

The pursuit of his fortune would continue after his retirement from baseball, and baseball would be a factor in Harmon reaching his ultimate goal. After the close of the 1913 season, Bob returned to northern Louisiana and purchased property at Homer. There seems to be a number of things that attracted him to that area. The site of his greatest baseball achievement, the near perfect game he pitched in 1909, was at nearby Shreveport. He loved the beauty of the rolling hills of northwest Louisiana, and he had a cousin who lived in Shreveport. There were signs that oil might lie beneath the surface of the land around Homer, and that could lead to handsome future earnings after his baseball career was concluded if the timing were right.

Harmon became friends with several individuals around Homer as he and Beulah made their off-season home there. When he closed his professional baseball career in 1920, he and two friends were already in the process of pooling their resources in the development of the Homer and Haynesville oil fields. They soon expanded the scope of their drilling to include development of an oil field near El Dorado, Arkansas. Their investments occurred at the right places and at the right time. Oil was found and lots of it, and the market was ready. There followed an oil boom in Claiborne Parish as thousands of businessmen and speculators poured in, in an effort to get their share of the "Black Gold." The first year of the boom was accompanied by day after day of moderate to heavy rain, and Herbert H. Watkins would later describe it as "the year of rain, mud and mules." Mules were the transportation of choice in moving wagons loaded with casings, equipment, and other oil field necessities. Mud was knee deep in some of the streets of Homer. By 1922, the Shreveport *Times* reported that the population of Haynesville had increased 1,000 percent in one year. Amidst the frantic and successful search for productive wells, Wideman, Harmon & Chaddick were riding the crest of success. Bob Harmon's share of the highly successful venture was made possible, in part, by his baseball earnings. By 1922, in an advertisement in the Shreveport *Times*, the business partners proclaimed, "'Poor Boys but Good Boys'– Now in Millionaire Class." Bob Harmon had indeed found his fortune.

However, he was not comfortable with his financial resources tied up in one relatively new industry, successful as it had been. More than anything else he yearned to own land and become what he called a "dirt farmer." So, in 1922, he liquidated most of his oil investments and purchased a large acreage in northeast Louisiana south of Monroe on the banks of the Ouachita River. He had admired the beauty of the river since the first time he saw it. The property would eventually be developed into Roselawn Plantation, covering 820 acres. Many acres would be devoted to row crops such as soybeans, cotton and corn, and a large dairy was created. It would also bear the name Roselawn and would become the largest dairy in northeast Louisiana. From that time forward, Bob Harmon would be known in southern terminology as a "planter."

Roselawn Plantation became a plantation of the typical southern style, numerous buildings with specific purposes assigned to them and numerous workers who also had specific assigned duties. The plantation home was a magnificent nine-room two-story mansion with brick columns and portico, a large library, and four bedrooms in an upstairs designed in the shape of an H allowing each bedroom to have windows on three sides. When purchased by the Harmons, the property had only a crude building made up of logs and boards. It was torn down and replaced by the magnificent house that Harmon personally designed. The connecting staircase was in the center of the house, which was situated hardly more than 100 yards from the Ouachita River. Grandson Jack Trost, Jr. adds that the huge home was the scene of many lavish parties given by the Harmons during the 1920s and '30s.

Roselawn Plantation prospered, and in the late 1930s Bob Harmon was recognized as "Louisiana Farmer of the Year." His dairy cattle won numerous blue ribbons at agricultural expositions around the state. The 1931 edition of *Who's Who in the Twin Cities* (Monroe and West Monroe) credits him with a herd of 150 dairy cattle, 90 percent of which were pure bred Jersey. *Eastern Louisiana, A History of The Watershed of the Ouachita River and The Florida Parishes*, circa 1939, says of Harmon, "As a farmer, dairyman and cattle raiser, Mr.

Harmon is regarded as an authority on the development of these enterprises, and because of his ability and splendid judgement, his services have been sought on many commissions and various organizations. . . 'Bob' Harmon is a man of energy and determination, a man who does things in a big way, and he enjoys the respect and esteem of a wide circle of fine friends." Nearly 20 years later in 1957, he was cited for the Farm Bureau Outstanding Service Award.

Harmon, now a true southern gentleman, was known for his generosity, frequently giving milk to the needy, especially to mothers with small children.

The Harmons had no children of their own, so in the late 1920s they adopted a daughter, naming her Jean. She would eventually bear them two grandsons, Bob and Jack Trost, Jr., and a granddaughter, Sherry Sherman. Jack Trost says that he and brother Bob made their home at Roselawn Plantation for nearly 12 years after their father left them and his mother and returned to his native Chicago. During that time, the two boys affectionately called their grandfather "Daddy Bob," a name that is still used by the Trost brothers and other Harmon descendants.

Trost says that during the 12 years he and his brother lived at Roselawn Plantation, they were trained in good manners and proper ethics. He quoted his grandfather as telling him, "Son, if you can't say anything good about someone, don't say anything at all." Other revealing bits of advice included "A handshake is a man's word" and "Speak only when no one else is speaking."

Trost recalls Harmon's love of the West, especially Arizona and New Mexico, which he called his "native land." He accompanied his grandfather on several trips to the region, the first when Trost was just five years old.

After retiring from professional baseball in 1920, Bob Harmon's interest in the game remained strong. He is credited with founding the Little League in Monroe in about 1950 and

serving as coach and manager of the Palace team as it won five consecutive Louisiana Little League championships. The team was named for the Palace Building, the highest building in Monroe. He also directed or participated in various baseball clinics for several years, teaching the fundamentals of the game to young ball players of the Monroe area.

Other interests and pastimes included playing the fiddle, which he continued to do until a 1946 accident burned his hands and dulled the sensitivity of his fingers. Harmon loved to play pool and had an expensive pool table in the library of his spacious home. His grandson, Jack Trost, believes that he had a close friendship with billiards legend Willie Mosconi. He also served as referee for wrestling and boxing matches in Monroe during the 1920s.

Beginning in 1956, he became enamored with Lincoln Continental automobiles. It started as he discussed purchasing a new automobile at a Cadillac dealership in Monroe but was deflected by the salesman who saw the tobacco burns on his shirt (Bob was a pipe smoker.). The salesman felt such an unkempt appearance was an indication he didn't have the finances to purchase a new automobile. An effort was made to sell him a used one, but Bob calmly strode across the street to a Lincoln/Mercury dealer (whom he knew) and wrote a personal check for a new Lincoln Continental. He would drive Lincoln Continentals for the rest of his life.

Chapter 8

REAL ESTATE, BEULAH & THE FIRE

Bob Harmon became an astute businessman soon after he left baseball. His successes in the oil industry attest to that, but his early bailout in favor of purchasing land is an indication of his conservative approach in search of financial stability. In the middle 1940s, he purchased 1,000 acres of undeveloped land along the east side of U.S. Highway 165 (earlier known as the Columbia Road) about two miles south of his Roselawn Plantation, paying only one dollar per acre. Feeling that it had possibilities for future development, he began the slow process of clearing away a small part of the brush by himself. Large scale clearing would be required later. On Good Friday, 1946, he was burning some of the stacked brush using gasoline to ignite diesel fuel that had been spread on the brush pile. Some of the gasoline fumes reached the flames causing a fiery explosion and setting Harmon's clothing ablaze. He struggled to extricate himself from the burning clothing and finally succeeded, but not before he suffered burns over 30 percent of his body. Totally naked and in great pain, he got in his truck and drove the two miles home. From there, he was immediately taken to St. Francis Hospital in Monroe where he spent two months in recuperation.

Eventually, developers approached him about the land and made an offer to purchase it. After some negotiation, Bob agreed to sell the entire parcel for $100 an acre, netting him a handsome profit of $99 per acre. The site would eventually become a subdivision named Charmingdale, and about 30 homes were built. Ambitious plans included the construction of a private airport, but this progressed only to the point of clearing space for the runway. Soon, Charmingdale fell onto hard times, and the developer eventually declared bankruptcy. Today, Charmingdale contains only a few houses, all in deteriorating condition. Whether or not Bob Harmon sensed the lack of wisdom in following through with a housing development project or was just the recipient of pure good luck will never be known. In either case, the end result was a remarkable rate of return on his original investment.

A unique sidelight of the accident in which Harmon was severely burned was the burning of his wallet containing a lifetime pass to National League games that had been accorded him and other retired league players in 1935. The passes were granted to those players who had at least 10 years in professional baseball. Two months after he had recovered from his burns he mailed a handwritten letter to National League President Ford Frick, explaining the accident and asking that a duplicate pass be issued. The request was quickly granted.

Bob Harmon was involved in other real estate ventures and during the later years of his life bought or sold properties on nearly an annual basis. Records in the Division of Conveyances in the Ouachita Parish Courthouse show him recording land purchases in 1925, 1929, 1938, 1946, 1947, 1948, 1949, 1950, 1952, 1953, 1955, 1959, and 1960. It seems plausible that the many real estate transactions in which he engaged added significantly to the growing Harmon wealth.

His foster father, O. E. "Ellie" Harmon, died in August 1940, succumbing to the progressive ravages of Parkinson's Disease at the age of 85. After the funeral, Bob took his foster mother, Viola, back to Louisiana where she lived with him and Beulah at Roselawn Plantation until her death in October 1946. Viola's body was returned to Liberal, Missouri for funeral services and burial next to Ellie in the Liberal City Cemetery.

It is interesting to note that Beulah did not make the trip to Liberal for Viola'a funeral. This seems to suggest that a distance had developed between Bob and Beulah, one that would remain for many years. A distant cousin who lived in Liberal during the 1930s and '40s says that Bob visited relatives there several times, but Beulah was never with him. He was always accompanied by daughter, Jean. She was also his traveling companion on several trips into the western states. Grandson Jack Trost confirms the existence of the gulf between the two when he says that he never saw any display of affection between his grandparents during his 12 years of living at Roselawn. Beulah did accompany him on what is believed to have been Bob Harmon's last visit to the town of his birth in 1959 when they visited his favorite cousin, Grace Noyes Pinkerton.

Trost describes Beulah Harmon as an elegant lady who loved family gatherings. Bob also loved family gatherings but reveled in all social occasions, events in which Beulah felt uncomfortable. Trost's son, Trey (Jack, III), calls her his "$2 Grandma" because she always gave him a $2 bill every time she saw him. She also had a sack of lemon drops waiting for him every time he visited Roselawn.

Beulah had a brother who was well known in St. Louis. Bud Mysonhimer was a chef for a number of restaurants in St. Louis owned by Anheiser-Busch. This was decades before Anheiser-Busch purchased the St. Louis Cardinal franchise.

Chapter 9

MISSED OPPORTUNITIES & FAREWELL

As successful as Bob Harmon was in his business ventures, operating Roselawn Dairy and buying and selling real estate, there is little doubt that he could have amassed an even greater fortune had he seized on other business opportunities that came his way. He was an almost daily figure at the downtown stock exchange in Monroe, and his intense love of billiards also required time that he was willing to give. He was content with his station in life. He realized that many years before, even when he was in the process of developing Roselawn Plantation. The *Agricultural Development Bulletin* quoted him in 1925, "I'm realizing an ambition I had for years before I quit baseball, and I'm getting out of it even more fun than I expected. I'd not go back to the old life - grand as it was - for any amount of money."

By far, the business opportunity he declined that proved to be most successful came his way in the late 1940s. A friend, Hank Biedenharn, Sr., approached him about creating an air freight company, something that at that time seemed to offer some possibilities of growth but may have been a bit before its time. Bob declined the offer in favor of continuing in his current business interests. The idea went forward, and eventually Delta Air Freight was formed, later growing into Delta Air Lines.

As Bob Harmon reached his 60s, he began to slow his pace of life. Parts of the plantation were sold, and the dairy operation was finally closed. He would still buy and sell on the stock market, and real estate remained an active interest. Of course, billiards would always remain a passion.

On the evening of November 27, 1961, he was finishing the day in his favorite manner, reading in bed. It was around nine o'clock. A sharp pain developed in his chest and wouldn't go away as he hoped it would. He called to Beulah for help, and she quickly summoned an ambulance. At 10:40 p.m., he was pronounced dead at St. Francis Hospital in Monroe. Bob Harmon was 74. Grandson Jack Trost is absolutely certain that Daddy Bob did not die at St. Francis Hospital; he surrendered his remarkable trip through life at his favorite place on earth, his beloved Roselawn Plantation.

The following day a front page story in the Monroe *News-Star* proclaimed, "Big Leaguer Harmon Dies" and a sub-headline read, "Ex-Pitcher Of Cardinals Was Prominent Here." The three-column story by Executive Sports Editor Paul Martin reviewed his entire baseball career and his involvement in the activities of Ouachita Parish for nearly 40 years. It quoted Harmon as modestly always calling himself a "novice" in baseball. It made it clear that "From Missouri orphan to the major leagues to Louisiana millionaire, Bob Harmon touched all the bases."

Epilogue

Beulah continued to live at Roselawn until her death in 1974 and was buried beside her husband of 48 years in Monroe's Riverview Burial Park. For a period of time afterward, the remaining part of the plantation was turned into a hog farm with grandsons Jack and Bob helping in the operation.

In 1975, Jean gained ownership and eventually converted the plantation home into a fine restaurant. She named it "Plantation Estates," and pictures from her father's baseball career adorned the walls. For nearly a year the enterprise did quite well, but it was closed when road construction in the area made it difficult to reach, and the clientele dwindled.

By 1979, only 65 acres of the original 820-acre plantation remained, and it included the mansion. Jean sold that parcel to Leonard W. Bunch on April 27 of that year.

The plantation home remained vacant for a number of years and slowly fell into decay. It was rented to an individual for a few years in the 1990s, but the deterioration was allowed to continue. The Spanish tile roof developed numerous cracks and was finally replaced. Later, the roof was heavily damaged when a large nearby pecan tree fell onto it. Some of the windows were broken, and the front door hung partially open on rusting hinges.

On September 23, 2003, the house and approximately two acres were purchased by Laura Louise Twiner and occupied by Mrs. Twiner's daughter and husband, Sherry and Kenneth Nelson. The Nelsons declared their intentions of restoring the structure to its appearance of the Roselawn Plantation years but admitted they had a difficult and costly task ahead of them.

When this book was virtually finished in mid-December, 2006, Great-granddaughter Beth Hart called the author to disclose that the Harmon plantation home is likely to be returned to family ownership. The Nelsons have conceded that they do not have the resources required to restore the structure and have been considering an offer from a contractor who wants to convert it to office space. In a telephone conversation with Mrs.Nelson, Beth said that her Uncle Jack would like to purchase the house and return it to Harmon family ownership. Mrs. Nelson was agreeable to the idea saying that it is only right that a descendent of Bob Harmon should own the structure once again and see that restoration becomes a reality. The verbal agreement is to become a written contract as soon as Jack Trost receives his settlement payment for loss of his home in Lake Charles due to Hurricane Rita in 2005 and agreement can be reached on a sale price. According to Beth, when she informed Jack that Mrs. Nelson was willing to sell him the house, he exclaimed, "We're finally going home." Fighting back tears, Beth said, "This is the best Christmas present ever."

Jack said later that he may seek grants to assist in the restoration if the house qualifies. Priority projects include replacing the Spanish tile roof, installing red carpeting as was in the house in the glory days of Roselawn Plantation, and restoring the beauty of the lawn. Also, he would like to see the house listed on the National Register of Historic Places.

● ● ● ● ● ● ● ● ● ● ●

There were many things learned about Bob and Beulah Harmon, their extended family, and their beloved Roselawn Plantation in conducting research for this book that didn't seem to fit into the manuscript. Still, these are things that ought to be passed on to the reader. There follows, in no particular order, a collection of these Harmon tidbits.

A fire occurred at the plantation house in about 1967, while Beulah was still living there. It started in a closet and destroyed some furniture. There was moderate damage to the house, mostly water damage. No one was injured.

During a visit to St. Louis, Beulah's hometown and site of many of Bob's baseball successes, they visited the St. Louis Zoo. Beulah felt that one monkey at the zoo had flirted with her. Consequently, they later imported several monkeys from Central and South America and released them at Roselawn Plantation. Since the monkeys stayed close to the house, Roselawn became known occasionally as the "monkey farm." However, when one monkey later bit Beulah, they were captured and given to the Monroe Zoo.

When Bob was at the peak of his career with the Cardinals, he returned to Liberal to visit his foster parents at season's end. He was shocked at the notoriety he had gained in his hometown when a large crowd gathered around him when he stepped from the train at Liberal's Frisco depot.

During a visit to Liberal after his retirement, he pitched in a game matching local married men against local single men on October 26, 1929. The single men won, 7-2. The *Liberal News* reported that the Harmon presence drew a large crowd.

Edward F. Balinger wrote in the *Pittsburgh Leader* in 1915,

There's a Buccaneer hurler named Harmon
Who pitches and also does farmin';
When he starts the pill whizzin'
That curve ball of his'n,
To batsmen, proves mighty alarmin'.

A house was built on 15 acres of land to the immediate north of the Roselawn home which Bob Harmon had given to grandson Bob Trost. Trost lived there approximately 15 years, selling it in 1978.

In the early 1920s, Beulah was robbed of $6,000 worth of jewelry during a visit to family members in St. Louis. She was traveling with her sister and husband on King's Highway when they were accosted by three armed robbers.

Following the 1911 season, Bob and a friend opened a wall-paper business in St. Louis calling it the Syracuse Wallpaper Company. With that as a financial safety net, Bob held out for more money from the Cardinals for the 1912 season, eventually signing a contract that provided for a bonus if he won at least 25 games. He won 18. Also holding out were pitcher Bill Steele and third baseman Mike Mowrey. The three finally reported late for spring training at Hot Springs, Arkansas, leaving St. Louis with Robison Field buried under several inches of snow. The wallpaper business eventually failed.

On April 26, 1953, Bob Harmon suffered only minor injuries when his automobile was struck by a Missouri Pacific Railroad engine inside Monroe.

The Cardinal team was aboard a New York, New Haven, & Hartford train enroute to Boston when it wrecked at Bridgeport, Connecticut in July, 1912. Only one Cardinal player was injured, pitcher Rube Geyer, who suffered a severely sprained wrist. Manager Roger Bresnahan and several Cardinal players were commended by the mayor of Bridgeport for their assistance in rescuing passengers from the wrecked cars.

When commenting on his draft status as U. S. involvement in World War I approached, Bob Harmon stated, "The first game of professional ball I ever saw in my life I pitched, and the first major league game I ever saw in my life I pitched." He was 29 years old at the time and beyond draft age.

Bob Harmon always referred to his mother-in-law (Buelah's mother) as "Grandma Dan."

Stories about the plantation home being haunted after the deaths of Bob and Beulah abound. Here are a few of them.

- In July 1998, Beth Hart (Bob Trost's daughter, Bob Harmon's great-granddaughter) took her 9-year-old son to the deteriorating house to show him where his famous ancestor had lived. They went upstairs to find all the bedroom doors open except the one used by Bob Harmon. Finding the door locked, she suddenly called out, "Daddy Bob, it's Beth. Please let me in." The door slowly opened revealing no one was there, but it was unusually cool inside even though it was a hot summer day. Thereupon, Beth and son quickly fled.
- Beth's husband and their two sons were walking across the lawn of the home in the autumn of 2000. They heard the crunch of additional footsteps in the fallen leaves near them and stopped to see who was there. The crunch of the additional footsteps continued, but there was no evidence of the footsteps in the leaves.
- A renter reported frequently finding the kitchen light (pull chain type) turned on of a morning and the pantry door open. In years past, Beulah would occasionally remove canned goods from the pantry and give them to some of the plantation workers without Bob knowing it. The same renter reported hearing footsteps on the central stairway of the house at night.

- An unpaved path led from the house to some of the nearby outbuildings that Bob Harmon walked on virtually every day that the plantation was in operation. Fallen leaves supposedly will not fall or collect on the path in the autumn.
- In early December, 2006, Sherry Nelson's daughter and a friend were playing upstairs when both reported seeing a figure with large eyes, long hair, and wearing a red dress. The figure or specter was in Beulah's bedroom on the northwest corner of the second floor. Later, Jack Trost confirmed that Beulah Harmon was buried in a red dress, and her eyes were noticeably prominent.
- On December 29, 2006, after the decision had been made to purchase the plantation house, Jack Trost, Beth Hart, and Beth's older son visited the house and spent the night. When the son prepared to retire in what had been Bob Harmon's bedroom, he found a window wide open. Since it was a warm and rainy night, he decided to leave the window open. The next morning it was closed tightly and nailed shut.

When Beth Hart relayed the news that her Uncle Jack was going to purchase the plantation home and the approximately two acres that surround it, she addressed the subject of ghosts possibly being in the house. "If there are ghosts in it," she said, "they are good ghosts."

While grandson Jack Trost was living at Roselawn, he found a $100 bill. After his grandfather conducted an inquiry and found that no one had lost any currency, he told Jack to keep it. Searching for a place to hide the bill, he rolled it tightly and carefully placed it in the barrel of a .45 caliber pistol in his grandfather's gun cabinet upstairs. Both Jack and brother Bob had access to the gun cabinet. To Jack's dismay, his brother took the pistol out for some target practice a few days later, and the $100 bill disappeared into a small cloud of confetti.

Great-granddaughter Beth Hart was born four years after the death of Bob Harmon, but she always marvels at his appearance in photographs from his baseball years. "God, he was a good-looking man!"

Evidence of the Harmon role as a leading citizen and developer in Ouachita Parish can be seen in the names of three roads in the southern half of the parish. Harmon/McDonald Road runs directly in front of the Roselawn mansion, and Harmon/Johnson Road runs along the south side of the Charmingdale development. Harmon/Alford Road lies in the southwest corner of the Parish just north of a fish hatchery. The Harmon Memorial Raceway also bears his name and was developed by daughter Jean and her son, Jack.

Bob Harmon served in many capacities in various organizations in and around Ouachita Parish during his life. He was a member of the Masonic and Odd Fellows Lodges, for 18 years chairman of the Agricultural Stabilization Committee for Ouachita Parish, a past president of the Federal Land Bank Association, a long time member of the Beouf Soil Conservation District (for 15 years its president), past president of the Louisiana Dairymen's Association, chairman of the War Board (selective service) during World War II, and active member of the Ouachita Parish Farm Bureau.

Bob Harmon's biological father, Frank Greene, died in Pennsylvania in 1893. His place of burial is unknown.

When Bob was in elementary school in Chehalis, Washington in about 1895, foster father O. E. Harmon wrote the following poem for him to read in a Christmas program.

Good old Christmas is here again!
Dear Mr. Santa Claus, where have you been?
O'er north and south, o'er east and west,
You've traveled hard and it's time to rest.

Please stop at our house a little while,
And let us see your generous smile;
We have a good place to shelter your rig,
And our hearts are well as our stockings are big.

Unload your presents so rich and so fine;
Fill up the stockings, be sure and fill mine;
And as you journey the wide world o'er,
O do not forget the sad and the poor.

If down the chimney you try to crawl,
And you find it small - a little too small,
Just knock at the door with a great big grin,
We'll open the door and let you in.

Bob Harmon's picture appears in the St. Louis Cardinal Hall of Fame.

Daughter Jean Harmon died on June 5, 1999, in Houston, Texas at the age of 72.

As this book neared completion, Jack Trost declared his intention of changing his surname to Harmon. "As his nearest living relative," he said, "it's only fitting that I should bear his name."

Bob Harmon died more than 45 years ago as this book is being written. He is still remembered by the older residents of Monroe as a prosperous and generous businessman and planter who just happened to be an outstanding professional baseball player. Hardly anyone in his birthplace of Liberal, Missouri remembers anything about him unless they are baseball history buffs. An exception is anyone in that community bearing the surnames of Noyes or Bryant. They are all distant relatives of Bob Harmon and know that somewhere in their family tree, there was a famous baseball player.

SOURCES

Chapter 1

Who's Who in the Twin Cities, 1931 (Monroe, La. and West
Monroe, La.), published by H. H. Brinsmade
"Liberal High School Records," 1900-1910, courtesy of
Drenda Farrell
The Story of Liberal, Missouri by O. E. Harmon
(Biographical Sketch added by J. P. Moore)
Nancy Bryant Benton, Tulsa, Okla.

Chapter 2

Nancy Bryant Benton
Evermore Genealogies, Noyes-Brewer and associated
families
Recorder of Deeds, Barton County, Mo.
Fritts Studio, Liberal, Mo. (photograph courtesy of
Jack Trost)
"Liberal High School Records," 1900-1910
Barton County, Mo. Historical Society (microfilm of
Lamar *Democrat*, Aug. 27, 1940)

Chapter 3

Baseball Hall of Fame and Museum, Cooperstown, N. Y.
Who's Who in the Twin Cities, 1931
Sherry Nelson, Monroe, La.
Ouachita Parish Public Library, Monroe, La. (microfilm of
Monroe *News Star*, Nov. 28, 1961)
Baseball-Reference.com/bullpen/BobHarmon

Chapter 4

Baseball Hall of Fame and Museum
Shreve Memorial Library, Shreveport, La. (microfilm of
     Shreveport *Times*, May 11, 1909)
Evermore Genealogies, Noyes-Brewer and associated
     families
Sherry Nelson
Jack Trost, Lake Charles, La.
Baseball-Reference.com

Chapter 5

Baseball-Almanac.com/players
Baseballlibrary.com/ballplayers
Wikipedia.org
Cardinals Hall of Fame and Museum
Baseball-Reference.com/players/quotes (*Sporting News*)
Baseball Hall of Fame and Museum (St. Louis *Post
     Dispatch* quote)
Jack Trost
Steve Constantelos, *Total Baseball*

Chapter 6

Baseballlibrary.com
Jack Trost
Baseball-Reference.com
A History of the United States [Since 1865] by Frank
     Freidel
Retrosheet.org/newslt17.txt
Shreveport *Times*
Baseball Hall of Fame and Museum
Kansas City *Star*, Feb. 22, 1917

Barton County, Mo. Historical Society (microfilm of
  Liberal *Enterprise*, 1906)

Chapter 7

Jack Trost
Herbert S. Ford Memorial Museum, Homer, La.
Shreveport *Times*
Beth Hart, Lake Charles, La.
Who's Who in the Twin Cities, 1931
*Eastern Louisiana, A History of The Watershed of the
  Ouachita River and The Florida Parishes*, nd, edited
  by Frederick William Williamson and George T.
  Goodman
Sherry Nelson
Ouachita Parish Public Library, Monroe, La.(microfilm of
  Monroe *News-Star*)
Baseball Hall of Fame and Museum

Chapter 8

Jack Trost
Baseball Hall of Fame and Museum
Ouachita Parish Courthouse, Monroe, La., Division of
  Conveyances
Barton County, Mo. Historical Society (microfilm of
  Lamar *Democrat*, Aug. 27, 1940, Liberal *News*, Nov. 1,
  1946)
Nancy Bryant Benton
Jack Trost, III, West Monroe, La.

Chapter 9

Ouachita Parish Public Library (microfilm of *News-Star*)
Jack Trost
Baseball Hall of Fame and Museum
Agricultural Development Bulletin

Cover Photos

Front: Warming up at St. Louis' Robison Field, 1912
Back: Inside Robison Field with two of his favorite
  possessions, a new automobile and one of his
  many pets. 1912

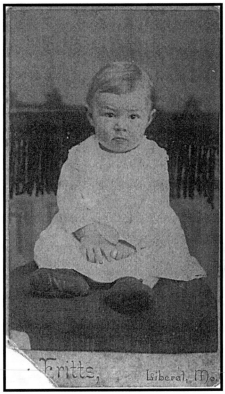

The earliest known photograph of Bob Harmon at about age one. Taken in Fritts Studio, Liberal, Mo.

In a house on this spot southeast of Liberal, Mo., Bob Harmon was born, November 27, 1887. Today, it is a soybean field but still owned by a distant family member.

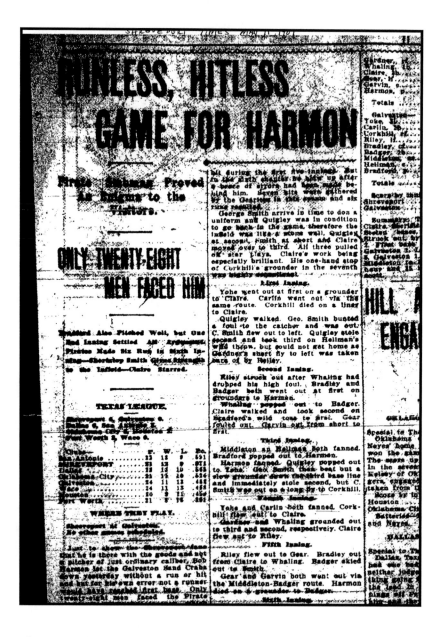

Shreveport *Times*, May 11, 1909, described the finest pitching performance of Harmon's career.

In his first year with the Cardinals as a 20-year-old rookie in 1909. Photo was taken in a Boston, Mass. studio.

Bob Harmon dressed to the nines. Studio portrait made in St. Louis, 1912. His ring
was not a wedding band but a multi-carat diamond ring he frequently wore. He
and Beulah were married in 1913.

Cardinals' Clever Recruit.

ROBERT HARMON,

Secured by Manager Bresnahan from Shreveport of the Texas State League on trial, less than a month ago, has proven a pitching find. His star performance was its 16-inning victory over the Giants on July 19 in which McGraw's team scored once in the first and twice in the third inning and was blanked by the youngster or 13 rounds. He lost to Brooklyn, 1 to 0, although but two hits were made by the Superbas, whose only tally was the result of a fumble by a St. Louis infielder. Bresnahan is not only pleased at the youngster's showing, but is confident that he will develop into a star.

A newspaper account in his rookie year, 1909.

Beulah Mysonhimer at age 18 in 1909.

Bob Harmon (right) gets acquainted with a newfangled camera while fellow Cardinal righthander Bill Steele looks on. Robison Field, 1913. Steele's grandson is currently employed by the St. Louis Cardinal organization.

Helene Hathaway Robison Britton, Cardinal owner from 1911 to 1917. She made Robison Field the official name of the Cardinal ballpark in memory of her father and uncle (Photo courtesy of Cardinal Museum and Hall of Fame).

Bob Harmon baseball card while he was with the St. Louis Cardinals.

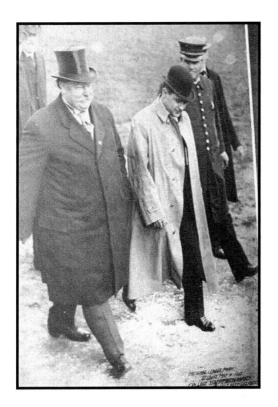

President William Howard Taft and his entourage entering League Park to see some good baseball, May 4, 1910. He was disappointed as the Cardinals jumped on Cincinnati pitching for five runs in the first inning on their way to a 12-3 win. After Cincinnati pitchers issued several walks, Taft left in the early innings for Sportsman's Park where the Browns played to a 3-3 tie with Cleveland in 14 innings ended by darkness. Cy Young was the Cleveland pitcher. (Photo courtesy of Cardinal Museum & Hall of Fame. Permission granted by St. Louis *Post-Dispatch*)

Roger Bresnahan, Cardinal player/manager, 1909-1912. He caught nearly all Cardinal games during that period. (Photo courtesy of Cardinal Museum & Hall of Fame)

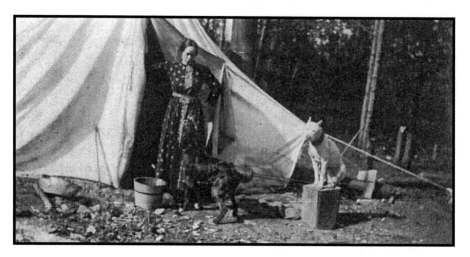

Buelah in one of the Harmons' favorite pastimes, camping in the woods. Circa 1917.

Harmon's friend and teammate at Pittsburgh was Honus Wagner, regarded by most baseball historians as baseball's greatest shortstop. Wagner, right, was much sought after for autographs. Circa 1915.

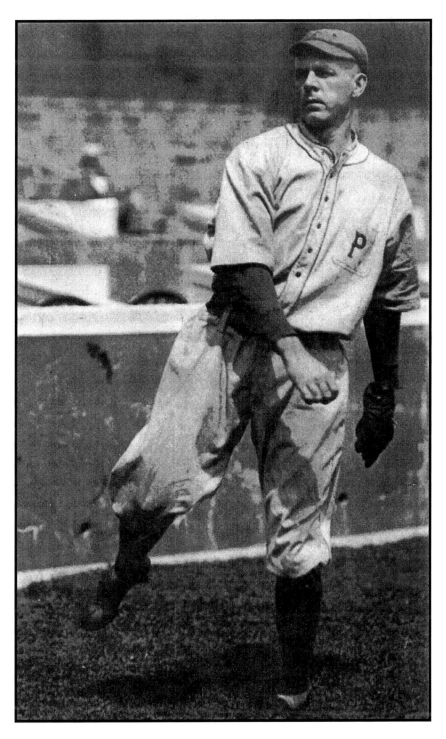

Warming up in the Pirate bullpen, circa 1915

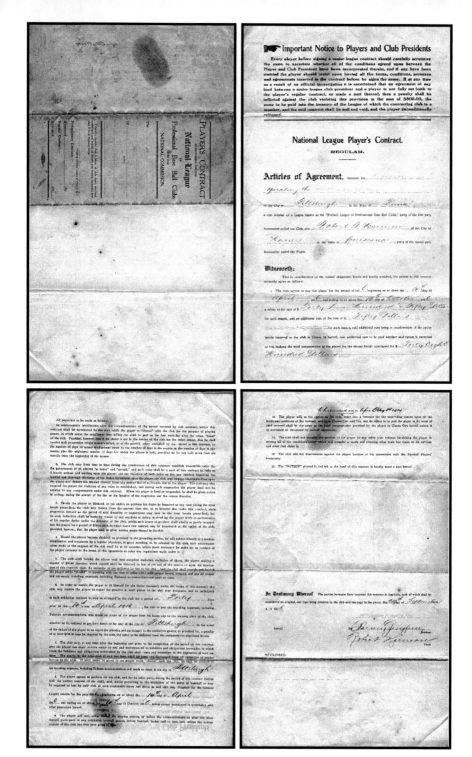

A portion of Harmon's 1916 contract with the Pittsburgh Pirates that covered the period of April 14 through October 14. It called for a salary of $4,750.

The photograph that confounds family members and the author. Where was it tak-
en? Obviously somewhere other than Pittsburgh's Forbes Field. In spring training?
On someone's lawn after retirement as a demonstration for friends? Family members contend there were no such fences (background) on Roselawn Plantation.
Bob Harmon retired from active play at age 32. What is his age in the photograph?
The dark shade of the uniform suggests a gray traveling uniform or maybe one
of deep blue or red. However, such colors were not worn by major leaguers until
decades later. Readers must draw their own conclusions on the story behind this
photograph.

Harmon the oil man with some of his associates and business partners in the Homer and Haynesville oil fields. Left to right, Gerrold, Yandell Wideman, Claude Chaddick, Bob Harmon (with tie), and Shaw. February 23, 1922. Wideman, Harmon & Chaddick became one of the most successful drilling contractors that operated in the Homer, Haynesville and El Dorado oil fields.

An advertisement by Wideman, Harmon & Chaddick that appeared in the Shreveport *Times* in 1922 quoted an oil magnate's description of the highly successful trio three years earlier, "Poor Boys, But Good Boys" and added, Now in Millionaire Class.

An oil derrick on the Harmon property, Homer, La., circa 1921.

The main building of the Roselawn Dairy, circa 1926.

Standing in a demonstration field of oats at Roselawn Plantation, May, 1929.

The National League of Professional Base Ball Clubs
R C A Building · 30 Rockefeller Plaza
New York

May 28, 1935.

Mr. Robert G. Harmon,
Rose Lawn Plantation,
Monroe, Louisiana.

Dear Mr. Harmon:

Receiving your letter was one of the most heart-warming features of the National League's presentation of lifetime passes to the stars of past baseball history.

Although Louisiana is a long way from the league, I sincerely hope that you are able to make some of our games this year, and undoubtedly get a big kick out of returning to the scenes of your former battles.

Sincerely,

Ford Frick

Letter from National League President Ford Frick in 1935 responding to Bob Harmon's request for a lifetime pass to National League games. The league had offered passes to former players who had played at least 10 years in professional baseball.

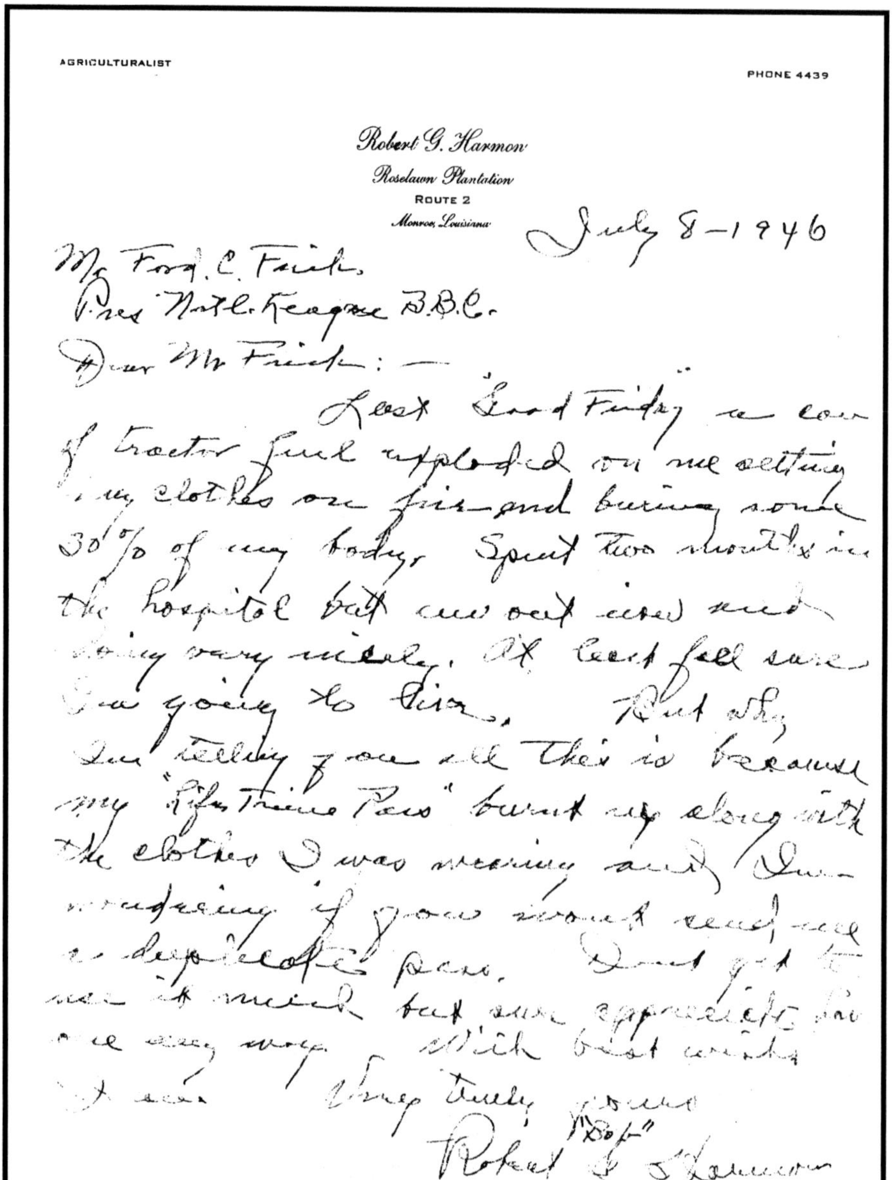

AGRICULTURALIST

PHONE 4439

Robert G. Harmon
Roselawn Plantation
Route 2
Monroe, Louisiana

July 8-1946

Mr Ford C. Frick,
Pres Natl. League B.B.C.

Dear Mr Frick:—

Last "Good Friday" a can of tractor fuel exploded on me setting my clothes on fire and burning some 30% of my body. Spent two months in the hospital but am out now and doing very nicely. At least feel sure I'm going to live. But why I'm telling you all this is because my "Life Time Pass" burnt up along with the clothes I was wearing and I'm wondering if you won't send me a duplicate pass. Don't get to use it much but sure appreciate having one any way. With best wishes I am

Very truly yours
Robert "Bob" G. Harmon

Bob Harmon's handwritten letter to National League President Ford Frick asking that his lifetime pass be replaced after it was burned in his near-fatal accident in 1946. Note his personal identification as an agriculturalist in the upper left corner of his letterhead stationery.

On a 1950 visit to the site of many of his great victories, 62-year-old Bob Harmon demonstrated his best pitch to young Cardinal catcher Joe Garagiola. August 30, 1950.

Junior Chamber of Commerce

Citizenship Award

To

Mr. Robert G. Harmon

In Recognition and Appreciation

WHEREAS, this individual, ever conscious of his obligations to mankind, our community, and our nation, faithfully promotes our civic and social advancement; and,

WHEREAS, in fulfilling this great obligation, he has become an incalculable force in the promotion of our community and national welfare; now

THEREFORE, be it resolved, that the

MONROE-WEST MONROE
JUNIOR CHAMBER OF COMMERCE

express, in this way, gratitude and appreciation for the inestimable benefits which have accrued to our community and our nation from his devotion and effort, together with hope that the future may witness his continued appreciation by the community.

Dated this ___6th___ day of ___April___ A. D., 195_3_

Garland D. Abell _____ _M.... A. Newhouse_
President   Secretary

The Monroe-West Monroe Citizenship Award given to Bob Harmon by the Junior Chamber of Commerce, April 6, 1953.

An annual old timers reunion at Shreveport honoring those who had played professional baseball in Shreveport. Bob Harmon, fourth from right, was the oldest member of the group at age 67. August 3, 1955.

Dizzy Dean, center left, was among those at the old timers 1955 reunion at Shreveport. As Dean spun his yarns in the Shreveport club house, Bob Harmon (upper left) listened in.

Harmon was deeply involved in Little League play in Monroe. Pictured standing at the far right, he managed another team to the Louisiana state championship as Monroe hosted the tournament. August 2, 1953.

Attending the National Association of Soil Conservation Distrticts convention in Omaha, Neb., February 5, 1953. (Photo courtesy of Omaha *World-Herald*)

Bob Harmon in 1959 as he started his 18th term as Ouachita (La.) Parish Agricultural Stabilization & Conservation chairman. The pipe was almost always present.

The Roselawn plantation home of Bob and Beulah Harmon in its heyday, circa 1938. Bob designed and built the house, and Beulah did the landscaping.

Roselawn Plantation home as it appeared in 2006.

Roselawn Plantation home, northeast view, 2006.

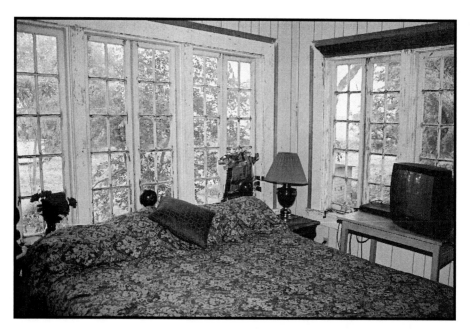

Southeast bedroom on the second floor where Bob Harmon died.

Being an avid Cardinal fan,

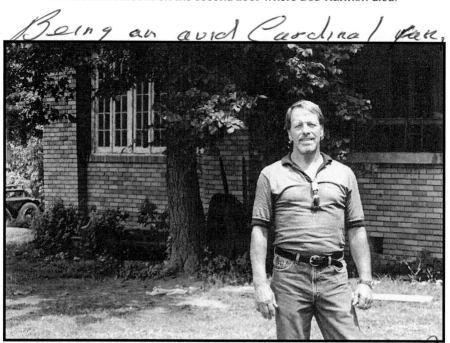

Grandson Jack Trost in front of the plantation home, 2006.

I'm honored you want this book

Best Wishes

Jack Trost Harmon

```
        GENE FULLMER COMPLETES HOME WORKOUTS FOR PARET TITLE BOUT--90
        AGS   SS722PMS 11/28..

   AGS 7 NES
   AGS 1 NES 1..

   NES1
        MONROE, LA., NOV.28(UPI)-- BOB HARMON, FORMER PITCHER FOR THE ST.
   LOUIS CARDINALS AND PITTSBURGH PIRATES, DIED LAST NIGHT IN A HOSPITAL
   HERE.  HE WAS 74.
        HARMON, WHO CLAIMED HE ONCE HELD A MINOR LEAGUE RECORD OF 146
   STRIKEOUTS IN 12 GAMES, WAS SOLD TO THE CARDS FOR $3,500 IN 1909.
        HE PLAYED FOR THE ST. LOUIS TEAM FOR FIVE YEARS AND THEN WAS
   SOLD TO THE PIRATES WITH WHOM HE ENDED HIS CAREER.
        AFTER HE RETIRED FROM BASEBALL HE CAME HERE TO DO FARMING AND
   DAIRYING.
        FUNERAL SERVICES WILL BE HELD THURSDAY.
                                      JP824PCS..
```

Teletype story from UPI on the morning of November 28, 1961, telling of Harmon's death the night before.

Bob and Beulah's grave markers, Riverview Burial Park, Monroe, La.

STATE OF LOUISIANA

CERTIFICATE OF DEATH

STATE FILE No. 17 218

1a. Name of Deceased: Harmon	1b. First Name: Robert	1c. Second Name: Green	2a. Date of Death: Month Nov. Day 27 Year 1961 — 2b. Hour 10:40 A.M.
3. Sex—Male or Female: Male	4. Color or Race: White	5. Married ☒ Never Married ☐ Widowed ☐ Divorced ☐	6a. Name of Husband or Wife: Beulah — 6b. Age
7. Date of Birth of Deceased: Oct. 15, 1887	8. Age of Deceased: Years 74, Months 1, Days 20	9a. Birthplace (City and State): Liberal, Mo.	9b. Citizen of what Country: U.S.A.
10a. Usual Occupation: Planter	10b. Kind of Industry or Business: Farm	11. Was Deceased ever in U. S. Armed Forces?: No	11a. Social Security No.
12a. City, Town, or Location: Monroe		12b. Parish: Ouachita	12c. Length of Stay in this Place: Years
12d. Name of Hospital or Institution: St. Francis Hospital			12e. Is Place of Death Inside City Limits? Yes ☒ No ☐
13a. City or Town: Monroe (Rural)		13b. Parish: Ouachita	13c. State: Louisiana
13d. Street Address: Route 2 Box 44		13e. Is Residence Inside City Limits? Yes ☐ No ☒	13f. Is Residence on a Farm? Yes ☒ No ☐
14a. Name of Father: O.E. Harmon	14b. Birthplace of Father: Mo.	15a. Maiden Name of Mother: Cora Noyes	15b. Birthplace of Mother: Mo.
I certify that the above stated information is true and correct to the best of my knowledge.	16a. Signature of Informant: Mrs Robert G. Harmon		16b. Date of Signature: Nov. 28, 1961

17. Part I. Death was caused by: Immediate cause (a) Acute Congestive Heart Failure — Interval Between Onset and Death: 11/22/61

Conditions, if any, which gave rise to above cause (a), stating the underlying cause last. Due to (b) Heart Disease, Arteriosclerotic — approx 6 Months

Due to (c)

Part II. Other significant conditions contributing to death but not related to the terminal disease condition given in Part I (a)

18. Autopsy Yes ☐ No ☒

19a. Accident ☐ Suicide ☐ Homicide ☐ — 19b. Describe how Injury Occurred — 19c. Time of Injury — 19d. Injury Occurred While at Work ☐ Not While At Work ☐ — 19e. Place of Injury — 19f. City, Town, or Location — Parish — State

20. I certify that I attended the deceased from 11/3/61 to 11/22/61 and that death occurred on the date and hour stated above. 21a. Signature of Physician: Charles M. Simonton — 21b. Date of Signature: 11/27/61

22. Burial [X] Cremation [ ] Removal [ ] — Date Thereof: 11-30-61 — 23. Name and Location of Cemetery or Crematory: Riverview Cemetery, Monroe, La. — Signature and Address of Funeral Director: Geo. H. Mulhearn, Monroe, La.

24. Burial Transit Permit Number: 37-405-A — Parish of Issue: Ouachita — Date of Issue: Nov. 27, 1961 — 27. Signature of Local Registrar

LOUISIANA STATE DEPARTMENT OF HEALTH, DIVISION OF PUBLIC HEALTH STATISTICS — DEC 4 1961

I CERTIFY THAT THE ABOVE IS A TRUE AND CORRECT COPY OF A CERTIFICATE DULY REGISTERED WITH THE LOUISIANA STATE DEPARTMENT OF HEALTH, BUREAU OF VITAL STATISTICS.

Andrew Hedmeg M.D. — ACTING STATE HEALTH OFFICER

Anthony Ciaccio — STATE REGISTRAR

JAN 21 1972

Bob Harmon's death certificate signed by attending physician.

Grave marker of Bob Harmon's foster parents, City Cemetery, Liberal, Mo.

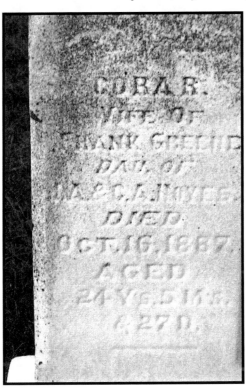

Weathered grave marker of Bob Harmon's biological mother, Cora Greene,
City Cemetery, Liberal, Mo.

The 1910 St. Louis Cardinals. Bob Harmon is fourth from left.

The 1910 St. Louis Cardinals.

The 1913 St. Louis Cardinals, Bob Harmon is tenth from right.

The 1913 St. Louis Cardinals, Bob Harmon is tenth from right.

The 1915 Pittsburg Pirates, Bob Harmon is ninth from the right.

The 1915 Pittsburg Pirates, Bob Harmon is ninth from the right.

The front page of a souvenir edition of the Pittsburgh Post, published as the Pirates' 1915 season opened. Bob Harmon is pictured on the bottom row, third from the left, directly under the buccaneer's hand.